Introduction

To the Preston family; Julie, Dave, Mark, Laura, David, Joseph, Lucy, Michael and Grace. Happy Christmas X

Magic Sparkles have been used on the cakes in this book. They are edible and safe to use on any cake decorating from fairy cakes to wedding cakes. They can be used on cakes, sweets, chocolates or desserts for a special touch.

Use straight from the pot or grind down to a finer glitter. To do this, either leave in the pot and stir with a teaspoon handle or use a pestle and mortar. To attach to cakes the surface should be tacky not wet - if too wet they will dissolve. Edible glue - see recipe below, is ideal although you can use water or alcohol. Their appearance is enhanced by good lighting - halogen or spotlights work well.

How To Use The Size Guide (CC)

On any instructions for modelling in this book I have used the Cel Cakes Size Guide. This should make it easier to produce proportioned figures. To achieve the correct size, the ball of paste should sit in the correct hole (size below it) with 1/3 of the paste showing out of the bottom and 2/3 out of the top (this does not apply to the smallest sizes). You will then have approximately the correct size ball of paste to shape.

Recipes

Modelling Paste

Either:- $1/2$ sugarpaste, $1/2$ flower paste kneaded together, or knead 5ml (1tsp) of gum tragacanth into 225g (8ozs) sugarpaste and leave for 8 hours, or knead 5ml (1tsp) Tylo (CMC) powder into 225g (8ozs) sugarpaste.

Mexican Paste

Mix together 225g (8ozs) of icing sugar and 3 level teaspoons of gum tragacanth. Add 25ml (5tsp) of cold water (taken from tap). Mix together, turnout and knead well. Store in a plastic bag and a sealed container for 6-8 hours to mature. The paste will feel very hard but will soften up easily. Break off small pieces and soften in your fingers. Matured paste will freeze.

Royal Icing

Place 30ml (6 level tsp) of merriwhite in a mixing bowl and gradually add 5tbs cold water mixing with a wooden spoon until free from lumps. Add 225g (8ozs) of icing sugar and mix until smooth. Add 110g (4ozs) of icing sugar and then add the rest gradually until the correct consistency is reached. Beat well for approximately 5 minutes. Store in the fridge, in an airtight container. It should keep for 4 weeks.

Softened Sugarpaste

Place the amount of sugarpaste you want to soften in a bowl. Chop up roughly and then gradually add drops of cold water. Break down with a fork or a spoon and mix until smooth and lump free. Continue until required consistency is reached. The first time you do this, be careful not to add too much water too soon. It softens quickly.

Edible Glue

This is easily made with 1 part Tylo (CMC) powder to 25-30 parts water. Place the powder in a bottle or jar that has a lid. Add the water, replace the lid and shake. There will be thick creamy white pieces in the water. They will dissolve and the liquid will become clear by the following day

Edible Supports

(for modelled figures). These are easily made from any left over Mexican paste. Roll out long thin sausage pieces and cut different lengths. Leave to dry for at least six hours. When used in modelled figures they are a safe alternative to cocktail sticks etc.

 GW00455113

NOTE: ANY SPECIAL EQUIPMENT USED HAS A SUPPLIER CODE. FOR EXAMPLE – SIZE GUIDE (CC) – SUPPLIER CEL CAKES. SEE ACKNOWLEDGMENTS PAGE 37 .

20cm (8in) Round iced cake on a 33cm (13in) iced cake drum, 950g sugarpaste coloured as follows: 320g red, 430g light brown, 40g dark brown, 25g green, 44g black, 80g white. 65g Marzipan, a little royal icing, Mexican paste, 12 edible supports 2cm long and 5 supports 4cm long (p1), edible glue, confectioners varnish (optional).

Paste Colours: **Red Extra, Black, Spruce Green, Pink, Paprika, Dark Brown (SF)**.

Dust Colours: **Camellia, White (SC)**.

Mouth embossing tool (Jem), Paintbrush size 3, sieve, no.1 piping nozzle, smoother, bone tool, Dresden tool, circle cutter 4cm diameter.

1 Colour 26g of Mexican paste dark brown. Follow the pattern on p34 to shape antlers. Push a 4cm edible support half way into each antler. Leave to dry.

2 Divide the sides of the cake into quarters and mark at top and bottom of side with a cocktail stick. A paper template can be made and folded into 4 to do this accurately.

3 Using the size guide (p1) measure 2 size 15 balls of red sugarpaste. Roll into sausages 16cm long. To finish roll both together with the smoother. Brush glue around base of cake. Attach legs to cake leaving a gap of 6cm for body.

4 Shape 135g of brown sugarpaste into a flattened teardrop to fit against side of cake for Rudolph's body. Attach opposite space for Santa's body. Make legs the same as Santa's but flatten at the top to lay over body. There should be a space each side for feet measuring 5cm. From 2 size 13 balls of black sugarpaste shape boots. Mark the soles with a Dresden tool. Shape Rudolph's lower hooves each from size 12 balls of dark brown paste. Roll a ball then flatten top and bottom making top narrower. Mark front with a Dresden tool. Attach hooves and boots joining together with a little glue.

5 Shape a teardrop from 135g of red sugarpaste for Santa's body. Attach to side of cake. Roll a strip of black sugarpaste and trim to 1.5cm wide. Cut to fit around body and attach with glue.

6 To support arms, push 3 edible supports 2cm long into top curve of cake from each side of bodies, with a gap of 4cm from body to first, then second, then third. Shape Rudolph's hooves each from a size 11 and mark with the Dresden tool. Roll sausages of sugarpaste for Rudolph's legs and Santa's arms each from size 14 balls of sugarpaste. Smooth to finish as before then brush glue thinly around top curve of cake. Press arms and legs on firmly. Shape gloves each from size 12 balls of green sugarpaste and point at wrist. Make a hole in sleeve, brush with a little glue then push glove in. Bend upwards and attach Rudolph's hooves.

7 Push an edible support into top of Santa's body. Colour marzipan with a little pink and paprika paste colours to get skin colour. Remove a small ball for nose and shape into a teardrop. Shape head narrowing slightly at the top and pressing in at eye area. Apply thin glue at neck and attach head keeping well forward. Emboss mouth and open up slightly. Curve the nose slightly and attach. Make hole for eyes then fill with balls of white Mexican paste. Mark lines from inside and outside corners of eyes. Dust cheeks and nose with pink powder.

8 Shape a beard from a size 13 ball of sugarpaste. Attach with glue then spread more glue thinly all over beard. Take small balls of sugarpaste and press through a sieve. Cut off with a knife then push the strands together and on to the beard with a cocktail stick. Attach a moustache and eyebrows using the same method.

9 From a size 16 ball of red sugarpaste shape a long cone for hat. Hollow out to fit head with the end of a small rolling pin. Attach with a little glue keeping well forward. Take end of hat to side and mark creases with a Dresden tool.

10 Brush a little glue onto Santa ready for trims and bobble. Roll sausages of sugarpaste, flatten a little, cut to size and attach. Place a bobble at end of hat.

11 Rudolph's head is 75g of sugarpaste rolled into a ball, flattened a little then narrowed towards neck. Attach to body. Roll front of face from a size 15 ball of paste, making a slightly flattened oval. Attach and emboss a mouth with a circle cutter then emboss the mouth tool at each end. Make eyes as for Santa, then mix a little white powder with water and paint a highlight into each eye. Indent area for nose with a bone tool. Roll a size 7 ball of red sugarpaste and attach for nose.

12 Cut a size 8 ball of paste in half for ears. Hollow each out with a bone tool then dust inside with pink. Attach to head. Brush a little glue at end of antlers and push into head.

13 Soften 40g of brown sugarpaste (p1). Place in a piping bag and cut a hole approximately the size of a no.3 piping nozzle. Pipe over Rudolph (avoid nose area) spreading out with a damp paintbrush then stippling to give the fur effect.

14 Using a no.1 nozzle and white royal icing, pipe the words 'Ho Ho Ho!' across the middle of the cake (template p34). Colour a little red then overpipe. When figures have dried 3 coats of confectioners varnish can be applied to hooves, antlers, boots and belt.

Oh Christmas Tree

20cm x 15cm (8in x 6in) Oval rich rich fruit cake marzipanned and iced, 35.5cm x 30.5cm oval cake drum, 225g (8oz) Mexican paste, 500g (1lb 2oz) white sugarpaste, 225g (8oz) red sugarpaste, 125g white modelling paste (p1), a little royal icing, edible glue (p1) 1 pot of white magic sparkles, Trex, 60g (2½oz) natural marzipan, edible support sticks (p1).

Paste Colours: Pink, Paprika, Dark Brown, Egg Yellow, Red Extra, Spruce Green (SF).

Powder Colours: Brilliant Gold, Moonbeam Ruby, Moonbeam Topaz (SK), Dark Peony, Camellia, Brown, Black, Blue (SC).

Lustre Spray: Pearl (PME).

Christmas tree cutter (Jem), strip cutter no.3 (Jem), bow cutter (FMM), garrett frill cutter (PME), scalloped circle plaque cutter (Jem), star cutter from shepherd set (PC), piping nozzles size 1, 2 & 3, carnation cutters or circle cutters 5cm & 3cm diameter, veining / frilling / mouth tool (Jem), fine paintbrush, dusting brush, size guide (CC), pieces of sponge, new scrubbing brush.

1 For carol books roll out Mexican paste and cut out 2 pieces 4cm x 2.5cm and one piece 5cm x 3cm. Fold in half and dry over folded card.

2 Grease board and bow cutter with a little trex. Colour a little Mexican paste red then roll out without lifting and turning the paste. Cut out 35 bows and dust with moonbeams ruby powder. Leave to dry. Colour a small piece of Mexican paste yellow and cut out a star. Dust star with moonbeams topaz. Leave to dry.

3 Colour remaining Mexican paste green. Grease work surface and roll out paste, grease cutter and cut out trees. You will need one whole tree and 5 trees cut in half to give ten sides. Trim the trunk off the bottom of every piece. Place tree pieces on sponge to dry. Make sure cut edges are straight by pushing the size guide against them.

4 Shape a cone from 105g of red sugarpaste. Shape two cones each from 60g. Leave to dry overnight.

5 Ice cake board and immediately emboss with the scrubbing brush.

6 Roll out white modelling paste thinly and cut out the large choir boy's surplice using the scalloped circle cutter. Remove one ½ then cut a lace pattern with piping nozzles. Apply glue thinly around tip of body and attach surplice joining at the back with a little glue. Press the folds gently into body to fit. Repeat for small boys but use the garrett frill cutter.

7 Colour the marzipan for the skin with pink and paprika paste colours. Remove 14g and add brown paste colour for the darker skin. Use the size guide to measure two size 7 balls of marzipan for the larger hands and four size 6 for the small hands. Roll into teardrop shapes. The large sleeves are a size 12 ball of sugarpaste rolled into a sausage and then cut in half diagonally to give the shape. Smooth cut edge and point a little more. Make a small hole at top of cut pointing up the sleeve. Brush a little glue on to points on hands and push up sleeves. Mark a crease at elbow bend. Brush a little glue onto side of body and inside of hands. Apply a little glue along bottom edge of carol book. Push book into body then attach arms pressing hands onto book.

8 Roll out modelling paste and cut out 3 circles (or carnations) for each collar. Frill edge with the veining tool. Attach to top of bodies with glue. Push an edible support into neck.

9 Reserve a little marzipan for ears then roll a size 14 for large head and 2 size 12 for small heads. Roll until smooth then narrow a little towards top. Attach onto support. Open the mouths with the veining tool. Make holes for eyes with veining tool. Roll and attach small balls of modelling paste for eyes or pipe in with royal icing. Roll small balls of marzipan for noses and ears then attach. Press the pointed end of the veining tool into ears towards front.

10 Mix powder colours with isopropyl alcohol and using a fine paintbrush, paint eyes, eyebrows and lashes. Dust cheeks gently with pink powders. Colour 3 shades of softened sugarpaste (p1) for hair. Use a damp paintbrush to brush into place and style.

11 Colour some royal icing green and place in a piping bag. Brush a little glue thinly along base of complete cut out tree and push down a little into centre of cake. Support either side with sponge. Pipe royal icing down the cut side of 2 halves of tree and position into centre of tree on top of cake pushing down into cake icing. Repeat placing 2 tree halves into each quarter of the tree. Leave to dry.

12 Spray tree and cake with pearl lustre. Colour some modelling paste yellow. Roll out on a lightly greased surface and use the strip cutter to cut out ribbons. Dust both sides with topaz powder before twisting and attaching to tree. Attach with green royal icing. Starting at the top, attach in loops to every other branch, start a new ribbon on the set of branches below. Attach a bow where every ribbon rests on a branch.

13 Pipe a little royal icing on bottom of star then push into top of tree. Pipe royal icing roughly around base of cake then cover with magic sparkles. Attach each choir boy to board with royal icing.

Half of a 20cm (8in) rich fruit cake marzipanned, 28cm (11in) cake drum, 900g (2lb) sugarpaste, Mexican paste, 2 pots of white magic sparkles (BK), edible glue (p1), isopropyl alcohol, Trex.

Paste Colour: **Navy, Black.**

Powder Colour: **Silver (SK), Pink, Navy (SC).**

Lustre Spray **Pearl (PME).**

Snowflake set (PC), stars from Shepherd set (PC) 2cm (¹/₂in) closed curve crimper, mouth embossing tool (Jem), size guide (CC), large flat dusting brush, small paintbrush, new scrubbing or nail brush, cutting wheel (PME), Dresden tool (PME), bone tool, sponge pad, cocktail stick.

1 Roll out Mexican paste on a lightly greased board and cut out icebergs (patterns p34). Leave to dry on a sponge pad.

2 Roll out Mexican paste very thinly on a greased board and cut out 6 snowflakes. Take out the small pieces with a cocktail stick then peel the paste away from around the edges. Leave to dry on a sponge pad. Roll out Mexican paste again and cut out 1 large star and 5 smaller. Leave to dry then paint silver by mixing the powder colour with isopropyl alcohol.

3 Cover cake board with sugarpaste. To get the snow texture, press the scrubbing brush in repeatedly all over. Stand cake on the flat side and cover back and curved side with white sugarpaste. Colour 240g of sugarpaste navy with the paste colour. Cover front of cake and trim. Open crimpers as wide as possible and crimp around edge of navy sugarpaste.

4 Place cake on board. Spray iced board with pearl lustre. Spray from the sides and not directly from the front. You should

get a good shading effect up the front blue sugarpaste. Finally spray from the front if more lustre effect on the snow is needed.

5 Use a large paintbrush to cover the top curve of the cake with thin glue. Grind 1¹/₂ pots of sparkles finer (p1) and use to cover the top of the cake. Brush a thin line of glue around base of cake front and sides and press on large flakes of sparkles.

6 Push large star into the top of cake. Attach snowflakes and stars with a little glue. Place icebergs on a piece of kitchen paper. Rub navy powder well into a flat dusting brush then dust from points of icebergs downwards. Spray with pearl lustre. Brush a little glue very thinly along bottom edge then press into iced board.

7 For the large polar bear use the size guide (p1) to measure a size 16 ball of sugarpaste. Start to shape into a cone then bend the top over for the head (remember that polar bears heads are small in comparison to their bodies). Point slightly for the nose. Pull out a small tail at the back. Use a Dresden tool to press in and mark front legs. Pinch out a little at the bottom of each leg for the toes. On each side use the Dresden tool again to mark a curve for back leg. Pinch out again for feet. Use the Dresden tool to mark 3 toes on each foot. Press the mouth tool in twice to get this mouth shape. Add tiny balls of paste for the ears and press in with a bone tool. Add a tiny black Mexican paste nose. Dip the tip of a cocktail stick in black paste colour and mark the eyes. The small bear is a size 14. Softened sugarpaste (p1) can be brushed on to the small bear to give a fluffier appearance. Attach both to the cake board with a little softened sugarpaste.

25.5cm (10in) hexagonal iced cake placed on a 38cm(15in) iced cake drum, 800g (1¾ lb) sugarpaste, 220g marzipan, 75g Mexican paste, edible glue, 6 x 3cm edible supports (p1), isopropyl alcohol, trex.

Paste Colours: **Paprika, Pink, Egg Yellow, Dark Brown, Baby Blue, Black (SF).**

Powder Colours: **Brown, Black, Pink (SC), Snowflake luste, Brilliant Gold (SK).**

Clay gun, mouth / veining tool, no.2 and no.42 Bekenal piping nozzles, garret frill cutter, 2 large flat dusting brushes, no.2 & no.oo paintbrushes, taffeta effect rolling pin (HP), turntable (optional), size guide (CC), new dishcloth.

1 Colour 25g of Mexican paste light brown for the sides of the manger. Roll out then use the taffeta rolling pin for the last roll. Rub brown powder well into a flat dusting brush then brush against the embossed lines of the silk pattern. Roll the flat rolling pin across the dusted paste. Cut 2 strips measuring 9cm x 2.5cm and 2 of 5cm x 2.5cm and leave to dry.

2 Colour a small piece of Mexican paste pale yellow. Make 7 halos by rolling thin sausages, then bending and pressing ends together to give a circle with a 2cm diameter. Leave to dry.

3 Place royal icing in a piping bag with a no.2 nozzle and pipe a small plain shell around base of cake.

4 Weigh 65g of white sugarpaste and shape for angel's body. Lay against side of cake and mark an outline with a cocktail stick. Remove body. Mix 40g of Mexican paste into 80g of sugarpaste. Roll out a small piece and cut out a garret frill. Cut centre out (if not already cut) and cut open. Measure the size you will need for first layer of wing so it will fit 1cm from bottom of cake and dress markings, to 1cm above top of cake. It should be positioned curving out from markings so it will show behind the next layer. Frill edge with the veining tool then attach with a little glue.

Repeat on other side then add another slightly shorter layer that meets the outline of body markings. Attach dress between wings.

5 Arms need attaching before wings dry. Using the size guide (p1) shape arms each from size 13 balls of sugarpaste. Roll a sausage thinner at one end and 6cm long. Pinch a long hem down at hand end. Brush glue thinly along wing and onto cake to corner. Press sleeve into place and mark creases at elbow. Dust dress, arms and wings with snowflake. Make a hole to take hand.

6 Colour 150g of marzipan with a little pink and paprika (brown paste colour can be added to this to achieve darker skin colours, measure the size for the hands and head first to get the correct quantity). Each hand is a size 7. Make a teardrop shape, bend a little, brush point with a little glue and press into sleeve and onto cake. Repeat for each angel up to this stage.

7 Shape heads in marzipan from size 14 pieces of marzipan. Roll a smooth ball, narrow slightly towards top, then press in at eye area. Press an edible support into each angel down the back of dress leaving 1.5cm showing. Brush

with glue then attach heads. Emboss mouths, make small holes for eyes, dust cheeks with a little pink powder. Roll tiny balls for noses and attach.

8 Mix a little brown paste colour with water and using the fine brush paint eyebrows. Paint eyelashes with black. Leave to dry then roll balls of white Mexican paste for eyes and attach. Paint in blue or brown eyes then black pupils. Mix royal icing colours for hair. Use a no.42 nozzle to pipe different hair styles. While hair is still soft press in a halo at an angle from back of heads.

9 Measure a size 16 ball of marzipan. Shape into an oblong 9cm x 5cm, 2.5cm deep at the sides but make a hollow for baby Jesus to lie down the centre. Try the pieces of wood along the sides to see if they will fit together. You may need to remove or add marzipan to make them fit neatly. Attach with glue. Soften marzipan with a little Trex if needed to push through a clay gun. Brush edges of manger with glue. Extract marzipan through the clay gun and cut off with a knife placing around manger.

10 Roll a sausage shape from a size 11 piece of sugarpaste for body. Roll out some paste left from the wings into a long strip. Place dishcloth over and roll with the rolling pin. Cut into a strip 1 - 1.5cm wide. Turnover and brush thinly with glue. Starting at the bottom, wrap around body taking up a little higher at the top. Place body in manger securing with glue then attach a marzipan head. Dust cheeks, emboss mouth, make a tiny nose and attach. Roll tiny balls for ears and attach. Press the end of a paintbrush handle into each ear towards the front. Dip a cocktail stick into black paste colour and mark eyes. Soften a little brown royal icing with water and brush on for hair. Attach halo.

11 Mix isopropyl alcohol with gold and paint halos. Attach manger to cake with royal icing.

Santa's Present

15cm (6in) marzipanned cake, 28cm (11in) cake drum, 1.6kg (3½ lb) sugarpaste, 100g flower paste, royal icing, 50g marzipan, 4 edible supports 4.5cm long 3mm diameter, 3 pots of white magic sparkles ground finer (p1), Trex, confectioner's varnish (optional).

Paste Colours: **Red Extra, Black, Spruce Green, Egg Yellow, Pink, Paprika (SF).**

Powder Colours: **Moonbeams Topaz, Snowflake Lustre, Brilliant Gold (SK), Camellia, White (SC).**

Multi ribbon cutter (FMM), funky stars (Jem), strip cutters size 1 & 2 (Jem), mouth embossing tool (Jem), no.42 piping nozzle, dusting brushes, pastry brush, raw silk rolling pin (HP), size guide (CC).

1 Cover cake with sugarpaste and place on board. Emboss lightly with stars. Ice board then dust with moonbeams topaz. Brush thin glue all over cake with a pastry brush avoiding stars. Cover with magic sparkles.

2 Colour 60g of flower paste pale yellow roll out on a lightly greased board and cut out stars. Brush with gold powder then attach to cake with glue. Roll out long strips of yellow flower paste. Use the silk rolling pin for the final roll. Set the ribbon wheel to 2.5cm wide using the plain cutting and the stitch wheels. Cut out 4 pieces of ribbon to fit from the bottom of the cake up to top centre. Brush with gold powder and attach.

3 Colour sugarpaste as follows: red 105g, black 56g, leave 40g white then colour remaining paste yellow and green for parcels. Colour marzipan with pink and paprika for skin.

4 Push an edible support into each side of cake in the centre of ribbon, near the top pointing slightly down and forward. Leave 3cm showing. Pipe around support with a little royal icing. Using the size guide (p1) measure a size 12 ball of red paste. Pinch between your thumb and finger to flatten top and bottom then roll around the side to keep round. Lay on side and cut in half diagonally so sleeve will fit at the correct angle to side of cake. Attach over supports and brush end with glue. Make gloves each from a size 11. Cut a thumb then push onto edible support. Attach a sausage of white sugarpaste around join. Support with kitchen paper or pieces of sponge until dry if needed.

5 For legs measure a size 13 then shape and cut as for arms. Attach to side of front ribbon so they rest on board. Shape boots each from a size

14. Roll a short fat sausage, bend, pinch at heel and side of foot, then flatten at the top. Attach to legs. Attach a white trim around each.

6 Remove a ball for nose from marzipan. Shape head pressing in a little over eye area. Push a support into top centre of cake and attach head. Emboss mouth, make small holes for eyes then mark wrinkles from inside and outside corners of eyes. Dust cheeks with a little pink powder. From a size 11 ball of white sugarpaste shape a beard and attach. Roll 2 tiny balls of white flower pas;te and attach. Add a tiny ball of black flower paste to each eye. Mix a little water with white powder and paint a highlight in each eye. Shape and attach the nose.

7 Place royal icing in a piping bag with a no.42 nozzle and starting at the bottom and edge of beard pipe tufts. Work up and along until complete, then pipe a moustache. Pipe eyebrows.

8 Shape a cone of paste for hat from a size 15 ball of paste. Hollow out so it will sit over head then bend and mark creases with a knife. Attach with glue. Add a trim then a bobble. Brush boots with confectioners varnish (optional).

9 From remaining coloured paste make 7-8 parcels. Dust with snowflake. Colour some flower paste red, yellow and green then cut out strips on a lightly greased board using the strip cutters. Dust with snowflake then cut and attach over parcels. Use to make and attach bows. Attach parcels to cake with royal icing.

Sleigh Ride

20cm (8in) iced cake, 28cm (11in) cake drum, 450g (1lb) sugarpaste, flower paste, edible glue (p1), 10g marzipan, isopropyl alcohol.

Paste Colours: **Red Extra, Dark Brown, Spruce Green, Black, Egg Yellow, Pink, Paprika.**

Powder Colours: **Moonbeams Ruby, Snowflake Lustre, Brilliant Gold (SK), White, Gingho, Fuchsia, Camellia (SC).**

45mm veined three leaf holly plunger cutter (PME), mouth embossing tool (Jem), small holly from rocking horse set (PC), sieve, sponge pad, no.1 piping nozzle, bone tool, pizza wheel, a selection of painting and dusting brushes.

1 Place cake on board. Ice board and emboss with the small holly leaves. Mix isopropyl alcohol with the gingho and fuchsia powder colours and paint holly and berries.

2 Colour some flower paste green and roll out. Cut out 4 sets of holly leaves. Place on a sponge pad and press a bone tool into the centre. Lay on a piece of crumpled kitchen paper to dry. Colour some flower paste red and roll 12 berries.

3 Trace the sleigh pattern from p34. Colour 90g of sugarpaste red. Roll out a piece of this to 5mm thick then cut out the sleigh with a pizza wheel. Dust with ruby powder then attach to the cake slightly to the left.

4 Colour some flower paste pale yellow and roll thin sausages for legs under sleigh. Trim to 1.5cm each and attach. Roll a long sausage for the runner 16cm long and attach to cake making a curl at the front. Roll sausages of white sugarpaste and attach at top and bottom of sleigh. Dust with snowflake lustre.

5 Colour 52g of sugarpaste light brown. Remove 12g and colour dark brown. Using the light brown sugarpaste and the size guide (p1) shape legs each from size 8 balls of paste. Attach over edge of sleigh. Make hooves from size 5 dark brown balls of paste, flattening top and bottom attaching to the legs then marking with a knife.

6 Shape head / eye area from size 10 balls of paste. Roll a ball, flatten slightly then pinch thinner towards where nose will be then attach approximately 1cm from top of sleigh. Shape six antlers from size 6 balls of paste. Make a long teardrop shape then flatten and make a cut to pinch out a long half and a short half. Pinch and curve each side out. Attach tucking points behind heads.

7 Roll a size 8 ball for each snout. Flatten slightly and attach. Mark mouths with the embossing tool and tiny dots with a cocktail stick. Dip a cocktail stick into brown paste colour and mark eyes. Colour 6g of sugarpaste black. Remove 2 tiny pieces for reindeer noses and attach. Make a red nose and attach. Roll tiny balls of paste for ears. Hollow out with a paintbrush handle and attach. Push brown

sugarpaste through a sieve and cut off with a knife. Brush a little glue onto head then push hair from knife with a cocktail stick onto head.

8 Shape santa's boots each from a size 8 and attach. The trousers are a size 11 ball of paste divided into 2 flattened sausages. The coat is a size 13. Make a teardrop shape, straighten at the hem and attach. Colour a small piece of sugarpaste green. Make gloves each from size 7 balls of paste by shaping a teardrop, flattening slightly and cutting a thumb. Attach one glove on cake at side of jacket and curl up slightly.

9 Roll 2 long thin sausages of yellow flower paste then mark diagonal lines with a knife to look like a rope. Attach to front of sleigh, drape across body and into santa's glove then down. Attach trims to front of coat and boots. Shape arm from a size 10, bend at elbow and attach. Attach glove over 1st glove and trim.

10 Colour marzipan with a little pink and paprika. Remove a piece for nose. Roll a smooth ball then flatten slightly. Flatten further in eye area. Make small holes for eyes and mark a few lines at the side of each eye. Add tiny balls of black paste for eyes. Mark mouth with the embossing tool and add nose. Dust cheeks and nose with a little pink powder.

11 Shape a beard from a size 7 piece of sugarpaste. Attach then brush thinly with glue. Push white sugarpaste through a sieve and attach to beard. Make moustache and eyebrows the same as for beard. Mix white powder colour with a little water and paint dots in eyes.

12 Shape a hat from a size 10 and attach. Mark bend in hat with a knife. Add a fur trim and bobble.

13 Soften sugarpaste with water and using a no.1 nozzle, pipe a small plain shell around base of cake. Attach holly and berries to corners of cake. Mix isopropyl alcohol with gold powder and paint sleigh legs, runner and rope.

Chocolate Time

20cm (8in) Round chocolate Madeira cake, 1kg (2¼ lb) chocolate cocoform (SK), 28cm (11in) cake drum, apricot jam or chocolate buttercream, Mexican paste, royal icing, 4 pots of chocolate colour and 1 pot of gold magic sparkles (BK), isopropyl alcohol, edible glue (p1), Trex.

Paste Colours: **Egg Yellow (SF).**

Dust Colours: **Brilliant Gold (SK).**

2cm (½in) double curve closed serrated crimper, no.1 piping nozzle, funky stars (Jem), star set of three and small star set (FMM), flat dusting brush, fine paintbrush (size 1).

1
Colour a small piece of Mexican paste yellow. Roll out on a lightly greased board and cut out 24 small stars. Cut out 2 large funky stars, 1 medium and 1 small. Cut out 5 different sized stars from the set of three. Leave to dry.

2
Place cake on board and cover with apricot jam. Cover with chocolate sugarpaste. Crimp around top edge of cake. Cover the edge of the board with chocolate sugarpaste and crimp. Roll out a long sausage of paste, attach around cake with a little glue and crimp. Rub gold powder well into the flat dusting brush then brush onto crimping.

3
Clean the flat dusting brush then use to spread edible glue thinly around the cake side. Place the cake over a piece of greaseproof paper then cover the sides with chocolate magic sparkles. Grind the remaining sparkles finer (p1). Brush the iced board thinly with glue then cover with the fine sparkles.

4
Grind half of the gold sparkles finer then use to cover the funky stars. Arrange stars on top of cake attaching small balls of paste under some to raise above other stars. Attach with glue. Attach small stars randomly around sides of cake.

5
Place a little royal icing coloured yellow in a piping bag with a no.1 nozzle. Pipe the words 'Chocolate Time, Misteltoe & Wine' (template on p34). Mix gold powder colour with isopropyl alcohol and paint remaining stars and lettering gold.

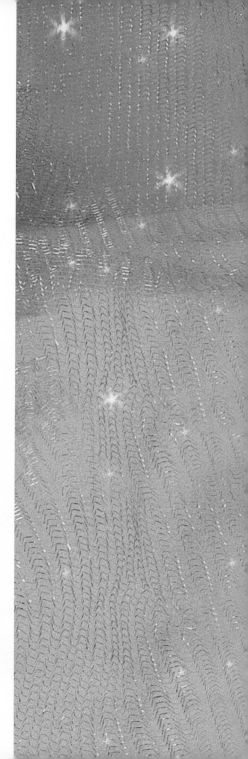

Shepherds

20cm (8in) and 10cm (4in)cakes marzipanned and iced in ivory sugarpaste, 30.5cm (12in) round cake drum, 10cm (4in) cake card, 600g (1¼ lbs) sugarpaste, Mexican paste, 50g marzipan, royal icing, soft light brown sugar, edible glue, 1 pot of white and 1 pot of gold magic sparkles ground finer (p1), trex, isopropyl alcohol, edible supports (p1).

Paste Colour: Gooseberry, Spruce Green, Dark Brown, Chestnut Brown, Egg Yellow, Paprika, Pink (SF).

Powder Colours: Snowflake Lustre, Brilliant Gold, Moonbeams Jade, Silver (SK), Camellia, Gingho, Brown (SC).

Buildings, trees and star from shepherd set (PC), foliage cutters from dinosaur set (PC), mouth tool (Jem), 1 piece of silver wire size 30, size guide (CC), no.2 & no.42 bekenal piping nozzles, rose leaf cutters medium and small from set of 3 (FMM), Dresden tool, scrubbing or nail brush, sponge pad, greaseproof paper, 2 pieces of dowelling, 2 lengths of size 24 wire, selection of paint & dusting brushes, small posy pick, non stick rolling board, small pieces of sponge.

1 Place large cake on board. Place small cake on card then on a circle of greaseproof paper the same size. Push dowelling into large cake towards centre back. Remove and trim so it will be level with the top of the cake. Replace dowel and position small cake on top of large cake. Colour a little royal icing light brown and pipe around base of small cake. Press soft brown sugar onto royal icing.

2 Colour 400g of sugarpaste gooseberry and ice board. Use the scrubbing brush to get the grass effect by pressing brush repeatedly all over icing. Soften a little of this paste (p1) and spread thinly where cake joins board.

3 Cut 4 pieces of wire each 11cm. Twist together and curve slightly but leave 2.5cm at one end and open out so wires form a cross. Colour some Mexican paste brown. Roll small balls, flatten slightly then thread onto the wires down to base. Paint a little glue between each piece. Continue until 2cm from top. Leave to dry.

4 Grease a non stick rolling board and the buildings cutter with trex. Roll out brown Mexican paste thinly. Cut out 8 buildings and separate with a knife. Leave to dry. Colour a little Mexican paste yellow and cut out star twice. Brush 1 star with a little glue, lay silver wire on top then press the other star over. Leave to dry.

5 Colour some Mexican paste green and cut out a set of palm trees. When the tree trunks are dry dust with brown powder colour. Using the foliage cutters cut out 2 small and 5 medium for tree tops. Cut 4 of the medium in half and leave to dry.

6 Dust edges of all palm tree tops front and back dark green and centres with jade. Colour a little royal icing brown and pipe between sections of tree trunk on wires. Spread icing with a damp paintbrush. Attach small balls of green paste to palm tree tips with royal icing coloured green. Attach small foliage tree tops over. Pipe a line of royal icing along bottom of set of palm trees and push into icing on top cake. Press brown sugar around base of trees.

CONTINUED...

7 Mix isopropyl alcohol and gold powder then paint windows on buildings. Attach with royal icing then spread brown sugar around buildings. Brush star thinly with glue and cover with gold sparkles. Push a posy pick into cake behind trees. Fill with Mexican paste then push in star wire.

8 Cut out one more tree top with medium cutter. Dust as before. Take the whole dried tree top that was cut out previously and brush with glue on wrong side. Lay top tree trunk wires onto leaves (wires at the bottom should be bent out of way). Now press the leaves you have just cut out over wires and press tree tops together. Pipe green royal icing down the centre of tree top. Place 4 tree halves into the icing with small pieces of sponge between to support. Leave to dry. Do not remove supports, turn over tree and repeat. Leave to dry. Cut a cross on iced board with a knife to sink wires into. Pipe a little royal icing under tree then push into icing. Pipe around the tree base then cover with brown sugar.

9 Colour some Mexican paste black. Roll a very thin sausage and cut 16 x 1.5cm pieces for sheep's legs. Colour some Mexican paste brown for crooks. Roll long thin pieces, 1 x 4.5cm and 2 x 8cm. Bend the top over for handles. Roll out white Mexican paste and cut out 2 medium leaves and 4 small. From 3 small balls of Mexican paste roll long thin pieces and press ends together to make circles with diameters of 1.5cm. Leave all pieces to dry.

10 For the sheep roll small oval bodies from Mexican paste. Brush tops of sheep's legs with a little glue and push into bodies. Push an edible support into the left side of one. Place royal icing in a bag with a no2 piping nozzle. Make heads, small tails and attach. Pipe curly coats and attach

ears. Pipe curls on top of heads. Add tiny balls for noses then dip a cocktail stick into black paste colour and mark eyes.

11 Colour marzipan with paprika and pink. If you want the darker skin colour brown can be added. Colour 50g each of chestnut and green and 12g of egg yellow with a little chestnut. For the large bodies measure a size 15 on the size guide (p1) and shape into cones. For the small use a size 12. Make size 5 hands for large figures and size 4 for small. Shape into teardrop shapes. Measure a size 11 for large sleeves. Roll a sausage 5.5cm long and cut on half diagonally to get the sleeve shape. Make hole in sleeves and push hands in. Mark creases at the elbow with a Dresden tool. Pipe a little royal icing onto the side of the sheep with the support. Push into shepherd's body. Attach arm around sheep with glue.

Bend other arm, brush hand and body with glue then attach arm to body with crook in hand. Small sleeves are a size 8.The shepherd looking at the angels should have his right arm and crook attached only.

12 The small angel's arms should have the hands in sleeves pushed upwards and brushed thinly with glue before attaching. Brush a little glue onto body, stick hands together then lift both sleeves at once and attach to body. Dust arms and body with snowflake lustre.

13 Roll size 11 balls of marzipan for large heads and size 10 for small. Roll smooth, then attach to bodies with glue and edible supports. Emboss mouths, dust cheeks, mark eyes with a cocktail stick dipped in black paste colour. Mix a little brown paste colour with water and paint hair on shepherds.

14 Mix together small equal pieces of Mexican paste and sugarpaste then colour for headdresses. Roll out thinly then cut 2 squares 7cm and 1 square 5cm. Check size against figure and trim if needed. Brush glue on heads and attach headdresses. Attach thin headbands over headdresses.

15 Colour royal icing for angels hair. It can be piped on with a no.42 nozzle or brushed on with a paintbrush. While hair is still soft press a halo in at an angle from the back of head. Mix isopropyl alcohol with silver powder and paint edges of rose leaves and halos. Brush glue thinly onto front and cover with magic sparkles. Attach to backs of angels with royal icing.

16 Stipple softened gooseberry green sugarpaste on top of large cake to place figures on. Attach shepherds to grass with the softened sugarpaste. Brush sheep's feet with a little glue and push into grass.

25.5cm x 20cm (10in x 8in) iced cake, 35.5cm x 30.5cm (14in x 12in) cake drum, 700g (1½ lbs) sugarpaste, 375g (13oz) red sugarpaste, a little royal icing, small piece of Mexican paste, edible glue, white magic sparkles ground finer (p1), isopropyl alcohol, trex.

Paste Colours: Black, Spruce Green, Red (SF).

Powder Colours: Brilliant Gold, Silver (SK), Red, Gingho, Camellia (SC).

Christmas Midi set (PC), snowflake cutter (PC), small Christmas tree (PME), reindeer cutter (PME), Dresden tool / stitch wheel (PME), no.1 piping nozzle, mouth tool (Jem), 2cm plain closed single curve crimper, assorted paintbrushes, size guide (CC), bone tool.

1 Place cake on board. Ice edge of board then crimp.

2 Shape red sugarpaste into a stocking shape – 18cm top to heel, 16cm toe to heel (Pattern on p35). Attach to top of cake with glue. Grease hands with trex and smooth the stocking.

3 Use the stitch wheel to run 2 lines of stitching across leg 4cm down from top. Run another 2 lines 5cm below 1st 2 lines. Make another panel from top of foot making the stitch lines 3.5cm apart. Use the Dresden tool to mark the knitted pattern from the top of the stocking, the ankle and toe areas. Mark lines down first (diag 1) then small diagonal lines between these (diag 2). Mark heel and toe with a double line of stitching.

4 Roll out Mexican paste very thinly on a greased board. Do not lift and turn the paste. Grease the small snowflake cutter and cut three snowflakes. Pick out the small pieces in the centre with a cocktail stick. Brush a little glue onto the back of the snowflakes and place on stocking. Cut out a reindeer and attach to stocking then a Christmas tree for either side.

5 Colour 95g of sugarpaste grey. Use the size guide (p1) to shape 2½ circles from 2 size 11 balls of sugarpaste. Attach to cake at top of stocking with a little glue, placing 1.5cm apart. Shape a 65g piece of white sugarpaste into a piece for top of stocking and attach to overlap teddies bodies slightly. Brush thinly with glue and attach sparkles.

6 Shape teddies arms each from a size 9. Roll into sausage shapes but thin at end to attach to shoulders. Attach from body to lay over stocking trim. Shape heads each from size 13 balls of paste. Flatten slightly when attached. Roll a size 7 for each snout, attach and flatten a little. Mark mouths with the embossing tool. Dust snouts with a little pink powder.

diagram 1

diagram 2

7 Dip the tip of a cocktail stick into black paste colour and mark eyes. Colour a small piece of Mexican paste black, roll 2 small noses and attach. Ears are size 5 balls of paste. Attach to head then press small end of a bone tool into ear towards head. Dust inside ear with pink powder.

8 Colour a small piece of sugarpaste green. Knead into this approximately 1/3rd of Mexican paste. Roll out on trex and cut strips 1.5cm wide. Cut one long piece that will fit across both teddies, 2 short pieces and a piece for the knot. Mark the knitted pattern as before on all pieces. Cut a fringe at one end of the short pieces and mark a stitch line across the top. Place long piece across both teddies attaching with glue. Attach short pieces then the knot over the top.

9 Soften some grey sugarpaste (p1) and place in a piping bag. Pipe all over teddies spreading out with a damp paintbrush to give a fluffy appearance. Do not touch the eyes.

10 Colour some royal icing grey and place in a piping bag with a no.1 nozzle. Pipe the words 'Christmas Greetings' on top of cake. As you pipe each letter tilt it slightly in the opposite direction of the previous letter. Pipe a small plain shell around base of cake. Pipe small stars randomly over cake top and sides. To do this pipe a letter 'K' then a 'v' on it's side joining the K.

11 Colour some Mexican paste red and green. Grease a non stick rolling board with trex and roll out paste without lifting and turning. Grease the boot cutter and the tree cutter then cut out 4 of each. Remove the star and pot from the tree. Roll out white Mexican paste and cut out 4 each of the bauble, bells, top of boot, pot and star on tree. Mix isopropyl alcohol with powder colours to paint in details. Attach white to top of boot and cover with sparkles. Attach pieces evenly around board adding the stars and pots to the trees. Mix isopropyl alcohol with silver powder and paint lettering, stars and border.

Eskimo Cake

20cm (8in) iced cake, cake baked in a 500ml pudding bowl, 35.5cm (14in) cake drum, 1.25kg (2lb,¾lb) sugarpaste, royal icing, Mexican paste, 20g (12oz) marzipan, 1 pot white magic sparkles ground finer (p1) (BK), piping gel, trex, 5 edible supports 2cm long (p1).

Paste Colours: Ice Blue, Rose, Violet, Black, Paprika, Pink (SF).

Powder Colours: Camellia, White, Speedwell, Teal (SC), Silver (SK).

Lustre Spray: Pearl (PME).

Mouth embossing tool (Jem), small curved nail scissors, Dresden tool, flat dusting brush, 1 piece of size 30 white flower wire, 2 white stamens, new scrubbing brush, size guide (CC), no.2 piping nozzle, cocktail stick, 5cm circle cutter.

1 Roll out Mexican paste and cut out approximately 12 triangles varying in size from 3 - 8cm in height and 1.5 - 5cm in width. Leave to dry.

2 Using the size guide (p1) measure a size 15 ball of white sugarpaste. Shape into a cone and flatten the base. Secure onto a lid a little wider than the cone with a little trex. Use the curved scissors to snip around starting at the top. Repeat with a size 13 ball of paste and leave to dry. When dry use a flat dusting brush to brush teal powder up the tree catching the tips of the branches.

3 Shape penguins body from a size 10 ball of sugarpaste. Colour small pieces of sugarpaste yellow and orange. Shape two feet and attach under body with a little glue. Shape a small cone for the beak then cut to open a little and attach. Colour a 5g piece of sugarpaste black then roll out and cut a kite shape for penguins wings (keep remaining paste for gloves). Check for size before sticking in place. The widest part is the tail end and the narrower end comes over the top of the head. Dip a cocktail stick into black paste colour and mark eyes.

4 Colour 35g of sugarpaste pink and 35g blue. Shape two cones 4cm high from size 14 balls of paste (1 in each colour). Wrap flower wire around the end of a cocktail stick several times. Take along the stick but leave it hanging a little loose then wrap around centre of cocktail stick. Take wire to end of stick leaving loose again before wrapping round the end. Do not bend wire down yet. Cut to measure 8cm long. Roll sausages of sugarpaste to fit around hem and up front of coats. Attach with glue.

5 Measure a size 10 ball of sugarpaste in blue. Roll into a sausage and cut in half diagonally. Mark creases at elbows with a Dresden tool and bend slightly. Make holes ready to take gloves. Shape gloves each from size 5 balls of black sugarpaste. Point at one end then cut a thumb. Push fishing rod into body. Push gloves into sleeves securing with a little glue then attach arms, pressing gloves together over rod.

6 For the mother, attach one arm only without the glove. Attach the fur trim around sleeve. Push edible support into body so 7.5mm protrudes. Colour 5g of sugarpaste violet. Shape an oval out of a size 8 ball of violet sugarpaste. Brush glue thinly across front of mother. Push body onto support. Place hand in sleeve then brush with a little glue and press onto baby. Make the opposite arm, pushing the hand in then adding the white trim before attaching to body and baby. Shape a cone for baby's hat from a size 7 ball of violet sugarpaste. Colour marzipan with rose and paprika to give the skin colour. Roll a small ball, flatten slightly and attach to front of hat. Cut a small mouth, add a tiny nose and mark eyes. Attach a white trim around face.

7 Roll 2 size 10 balls of marzipan and flatten slightly. Shape hats from size 11 balls of sugarpaste. Make cones then attach the faces to the front with the help of an edible support. Push another edible support into the bodies then attach the heads. Emboss mouths with the embossing tool, dust cheeks with a little pink powder, add noses and eyes. Attach fur trims.

8 Shape a fish in white sugarpaste and mark tail with a knife and scales with a piping nozzle. Brush with silver powder. Seal is a size 12 ball of grey sugarpaste. Point at nose and flatten underneath. Cut a mouth and open slightly. Brush with a little glue and add fish. Add a tiny black nose and push stamens in for whiskers. Make holes for eyes then add small balls of black Mexican paste. Mix white powder with water to paint a tiny highlight in eyes.

9 Place large cake on board. Ice the board and mark snow texture with a scrubbing brush by pressing in repeatedly. Cut two 5cm holes and replace white sugarpaste with thinner blue sugarpaste. Ice the small cake and mark ice blocks with a Dresden tool (measure and mark first with a cocktail stick). Place on top of large cake. Roll out white Mexican paste to a thickness of 4mm. Cut a piece 14cm long by 5cm wide. One long side will need to be trimmed into a curve, so it fits against the igloo, 4cm wide at both ends and 5cm in the centre. Mark ice blocks then curve and place against igloo. Trim if needed to get a good fit then secure with royal icing. Fill with kitchen paper to support until dry.

10 Pipe royal icing around all tunnel edges, top and bottom of igloo and around base of large cake. Using a flat dusting brush, dust speedwell powder from the top point of icebergs down the edges. Pipe royal icing along the bottom then press into iced board. Attach trees with royal icing. Leave to dry. Spray pearl lustre over cake, board, igloo, trees and icebergs.

11 Pipe a little more royal icing roughly along bottom of icebergs. Brush glue over royal icing around cake, igloo and entrance and cover with magic sparkles. Fill holes with piping gel. Place seal in hole. Attach penguin and Eskimos with royal icing. Measure the tip of rod to water so wire can be trimmed to correct length before bending.

Cake baked in a 1ltr pudding bowl, large muffin, 2 mini swiss rolls, 28cm (11in) cake drum, 1.7kg (3lb 12oz) sugarpaste, 600g (1¼ lb) modelling paste (p1), 60g (2½ oz) marzipan, 4 pots of white magic sparkles ground finer (p1), confectioners varnish (optional), apricot jam or buttercream, royal icing, 24 edible supports 2cm (p1), edible glue (p1).

Paste Colours: **Black, Ice Blue, Red, Navy, Eucalyptus, Dark Brown, Rose (pink), Paprika, Violet (SF).**

Powder Colours: **Camellia, White (SC).**

Lustre Spray: **Pearl (PME).**

Stitch wheel / Dresden tool (PME), button stick (HP), pastry brush, paintbrushes size 00, 1 & 4, strip cutter size 1 (Jem), mouth embossing tool (Jem), circle cutter 6cm, double curve closed serrated crimper 1cm, scrubbing or nail brush, 2 satay sticks, size guide (CC), scissors, ball or bone tool, sieve.

1 Ice board and mark snow texture by repeatedly pressing the scrubbing brush over it. Spray with pearl lustre.

2 Ice the pudding bowl cake and place on board slightly towards the back. Trim mini rolls to 5cm and cover with sugarpaste. Attach to board with royal icing. Roll a thin sausage of sugarpaste and attach with water around join of each leg to body. Press in firmly then blend with

a damp paintbrush to disguise the join. Use the size guide (p1) to measure 2 size 16 balls of sugarpaste for arms. Roll into sausages, narrow at shoulder end then flatten slightly. Brush glue thinly down sides of body and attach.

3 Trim the muffin if needed to make a ball shape. Roll out 250g of sugarpaste into a circle. Turn paste over and spread with jam or buttercream. Place muffin on icing then cover with the paste bringing excess paste to underneath where head will join body. Push 2 satay sticks straight down into body leaving 5cm showing. Pipe royal icing quite thickly where head will join body. Attach head making sure it is well forwards and not tilting back. Emboss mouth with the circle cutter and the mouth embosser. Make holes for nose and eyes. Leave to dry overnight.

4 Using a pastry brush and thin edible glue, brush all over snowman sparingly but avoid top of head where hat will be. Cover with magic sparkles. Tilt cake to let sparkles fall down cake easier but be careful not to tilt too far. Sparkles can be lifted on a flat brush to reach underneath curves of arms etc.

5 Colour 140g of sugarpaste black. Remove 2 small balls and attach for eyes. Shape boots each from a size 16 ball of sugarpaste. Attach and mark heel with a Dresden tool. Roll a strip of black paste to attach around the top of the boots. Colour a size 7 ball of paste with paprika and shape into a carrot. Mark lines with a knife and attach to face.

6 Colour 160g of modelling paste with ice blue. Roll out a long piece and emboss with the strip cutter. Trim the edges away. Emboss knitted pattern with the Dresden tool (diagram p). Cut a strip to fit around neck (25-30cm) and attach. Cut two shorter pieces but cut a fringe and crimp at one end of each. Mark knitted pattern and attach. Make a shorter piece (4.5cm approx), pinch the ends together and attach over joins.

7 Roll out blue paste for hat. Cut out a circle with a diameter of 16cm. Remove a ½ of the circle then check the size over the head to see if it needs trimming to fit. Brush head with glue and attach. Mark knitted pattern. Attach a size 12 flattened ball of paste for the bobble and brush with glue. Press small pieces of modelling paste through a sieve, cut off with a knife then push off knife onto bobble with a cocktail stick. Repeat until covered. Roll out a sausage of paste to fit around hat. Flatten slightly, attach then crimp.

8 Colour modelling paste as follows: red 20g, navy 60g, eucalyptus 90g, violet 40g, pink 90g, small piece of very light brown, small piece of dark pink. Colour marzipan with pink and paprika for skin colour.

9 Shape boots each from size 12 balls of paste. Roll a short fat sausage, bend, shape at the front, pinch at the heel, flatten at the top and hollow a little. For now, make figures off the cake board. Join together with edible supports and a little glue. For the legs, shape a size 14 ball into a slightly flattened square, narrow at leg end then make a cut to half way. Join to boots. Make the same size and shape for bodies and attach.

10 Measure around the body and the length to just above the boots. Roll out paste for coat and trim to size. Wrap around body to check fit. Remove and mark stitch lines. Brush bodies with glue and wrap coat around. Trim at shoulders

with scissors. Attach close to snowman with royal icing. If you can't get figures close enough, trim a little paste off boots with a sharp knife. Support until dry.

11 Make toggles for boys coat by shaping a tiny oval, attaching, then mark a line across centre with a knife, and a hole at the side with a cocktail stick. Add small balls of paste to girls coat then press with the button stick. Shape gloves each from size 4 pieces of paste. Point at wrist then cut thumbs. Shape arms from size 11 pieces, narrowing at top, flattening at wrist and making a hole for glove. Mark with stitches, attach gloves up sleeves. Brush palms of gloves and inside arm at top and attach.

12 Remove a size 8 ball of marzipan for necks and noses. Roll size 14 balls for heads. Flatten slightly in eye area. Push edible supports into tops of bodies. Attach size 7 balls over supports for necks. Emboss mouths then make holes for eyes. Roll tiny balls for noses and attach. Push underneath each nose on each side with a cocktail stick. Dust cheeks with a little pink powder. Brush a little glue onto supports then attach heads. Roll small balls of paste and insert for eyes. Press in with a large ball or bone tool. Mix a little water with paste colours then paint eyebrows, eyelashes and eyes. Paint a white highlight in children's and snowman's eyes.

13 Roll out paste for hoods. Cut a straight line to go around face then check the size to wrap over head. Cut to correct length, mark stitch lines – one from centre to back and two around front. Brush head sides and back with glue and fit hood over. Pinch towards back then trim with scissors.

14 Colour a little royal icing for hair. Pipe girl's hair around face then boy's hair shorter. Cut out pockets, mark stitches and attach to coats. Roll sausages of white paste and attach trims to boots. Make chidrens scarves as for snowman but narrower. Trim pieces to required size and attach. Confectioners varnish can be applied to snowman's boots and eyes.

25.5cm (10in) Petal shaped rich fruit cake marzipanned and iced in ivory coloured sugarpaste placed on a 30.5cm (12in) iced cake drum, flower paste, 4 pots of hint of lemon magic sparkles ground finer (p1) (BK), royal icing, edible glue (p1), Trex.

Paste Colours: **Egg Yellow, Red, Spruce Green, Gooseberry, Caramel / Ivory (SF).**

Powder Colours: **Brilliant Gold, Moonbeams Jade, Moonbeams Topaz, Moonbeams Ruby, Bronze (SK).**

Small veined 3 leaf holly plunger cutter (PME), small holly leaf plunger cutter (PME), small bow cutter (Jem), large star and small star cutters from shepherd set (PC), holly leaf rolling pin (Jem), 2cm single curve plain crimper, no.1 piping nozzle, large flat brush, paintbrush size 3, bone tool, soft sponge pad.

1 Crimp around edge of board. Dust icing on board with moonbeams topaz.

2 Colour some flower paste with spruce green and some with gooseberry. Cut out the triple holly leaf 40 times in spruce. Place on a sponge pad and press bone tool into the centre. Cut out the small holly leaf 35 times in gooseberry. Dust all leaves with moonbeams jade. Colour some flower paste red and roll 48 small berries.

3 Colour some flower paste yellow. Roll approximately 7 baubles. On a lightly greased board, roll out yellow paste, grease the star cutters and cut out a large star and 18 small stars. Leave to dry. Roll out yellow paste and use the holly rolling pin for the final roll. Cut out a pot (pattern p36). Cut out three presents – two yellow and one red in Mexican paste. Add strips of paste for ribbons to one present. Use the bow cutter to cut out 3 different coloured bows. Dust presents, yellow with topaz,

yellow with bronze and red with moonbeams ruby. Attach bows and dust with lustre powders as previously used on parcels.

4 Brush the cake all over using a large brush with edible glue, taking care not to miss anywhere. Place cake over greaseproof paper and cover with magic sparkles.

5 Colour a little royal icing ivory and place in a piping bag with a no.1 nozzle. Pipe a small plain shell around base of cake. Attach triple holly leaves into the 6 curves around base of cake.

6 Brush pot with brilliant gold and attach to cake with royal icing. Arrange holly leaves on top of cake in the tree shape before attaching with royal icing. Pipe a little icing into the centre of leaves around board and several on the tree and attach berries. Attach large star, baubles and small stars randomly over cake top and sides. Attach presents at bottom of tree raising to overlap on pieces of sugarpaste.

7 Mix isopropyl alcohol with gold powder and paint stars and baubles.

Rudolf in a Toy Sack

10cm (4in) square cake 5cm (2in) deep, 28cm (11in) cake drum, 1.5g (3lb5oz) sugarpaste, Mexican paste, 1 pot of Magic Sparkles (BK), edible glue (p1), edible supports (p1), isopropyl alcohol, confectioners varnish (optional), jam or alcohol depending on cake used.

Paste Colours: **Dark Brown, Black, Red Extra, Spruce Green, Egg Yellow, Ruby(SF).**

Powder Colours: **Camellia (SC), Brilliant Gold, Silver, Snowflake lustre (SK).**

Lustre Spray: **Pearl (PME).**

Mouth embossing tool (Jem), stitch wheel (PME), bow cutter size 1 (Jem), italic alphabet set (FMM), small blossom embosser from confetti set (PC), no.42 Bekenal piping nozzle, circle cutter 5cm, paintbrushes, scrubbing brush, new dishcloth – the thicker ones usually have a better texture.

1 Colour 40g of Mexican paste light brown. Remove 16g and continue colouring this piece for antlers. Measure 4 size 3 balls of light brown paste using the size guide (p1). Shape into short sausages for legs then push an edible support into both ends of each leg. Colour 5g of sugarpaste black. Each hoof is a size 7. Shape and attach to leg with a little royal icing. Leave to dry.

2 Roll a size 11 ball of paste for each antler. Shape and cut with scissors (pattern p36). Push an edible support into each antler. Leave to dry.

3 Colour some small pieces of Mexican paste in several colours. Roll tiny balls of paste into thin sausages then twist 2 colours together. Trim to 6-7cm then curve at one end. Make at least 5. Leave to dry.

4 Cover board with sugarpaste. Create the textured snow effect by pressing the scrubbing brush into the paste repeatedly. Spray with pearl lustre.

5 Stand cake up on side. Brush with alcohol if covered in marzipan or apricot jam if using a sponge cake. A size 15 sausage of sugarpaste should be added at the sides of the cake and then pinched out to give the shape for the sack. Colour a size 15 of sugarpaste black then roll out and over the top of the cake. Colour 300g of sugarpaste brown. Check the height and width of the cake. Roll out a long strip long enough to fit around the cake and add 1cm to the height. Place the dishcloth over the sugarpaste and roll across a rolling pin. Move the cloth and repeat so all paste is embossed. Trim straight and wrap around cake placing the join at the back. Push dried legs into sack, remove and pipe a little royal icing onto tops of legs then push back into cake.

6 Colour 100g of sugarpaste brown to match legs. Shape Rudolph's head from a size 16 ball of sugarpaste. Narrow a little where mouth area will be attached. Push an edible support into cake towards back and position head securing with a little royal icing. Roll a size 14 ball for the mouth area. Shape into an oval and flatten slightly before attaching. Emboss mouth with a circle cutter and the mouth tool. Dust cheeks lightly with a little pink powder. Attach oval pieces of white Mexican paste for eyes then small pieces of brown. Mix a little water with the paste colour and paint eyelashes and a line around eye. Mix a little white powder with water to paint a small highlight in eye. Attach a red nose. Roll small balls of paste for ears, attach to head and hollow out with a ball tool. Brush a little pink powder colour into each ear.

7 Colour some small pieces of sugarpaste ready for the toys. You can make any toys so they are suitable for the cake's recipients. To make the toys shown start with the doll. Her body is a size 12. Shape into the top half of her body, emboss with the small flower and attach to cake with edible glue. Make small thin sausages of marzipan for arms. Crease at elbows and cut a small thumb. Attach then cut small pieces of sugarpaste for sleeves and frill the edges with the frilling stick on the mouth embossing tool. Attach a small collar. Brush the dress and bow

with a little snowflake powder. The head is a size 12 ball of marzipan. Attach with an edible support, emboss mouth, dust cheeks, add a small nose and mark eyes with a cocktail stick dipped in black paste colour. Colour a little royal icing and pipe hair with a no.42 nozzle.

8 Colour a little Mexican paste pink. Roll out on a greased board and cut out the bow. Join pieces together with a little glue as you place them on doll's head.

9 The car is only the front half. Shape from a size 11 piece of sugarpaste. Mark window, doors etc with a Dresden tool. Add a bumper, lights and tyres. Paint silver by mixing powder colour with isopropyl alcohol.

10 To make the teddy shape body from a size 12 ball of sugarpaste. Thin towards top then attach to cake with glue. Attach arms each shaped from size 7 balls of paste. Legs are size 10. Bend to shape a foot pinching at heel. Mark arms and legs with a Dresden tool and the stitch wheel. Add a small tail. The head is a size 12 ball of paste. Add a snout and small balls of paste for the ears. Press a small ball tool into ears. Dust cheeks, mark eyes with a cocktail stick and add a small nose. The duck just has a head which is a size 12 ball of paste attached behind the teddy. Attach a small beak and mark the eyes with a cocktail stick.

11 Soften some brown sugarpaste with water (p1) and place in a piping bag. Pipe over Rudolph spreading with a damp paintbrush then stipple to give a fur effect. Push antlers into head. Attach candy sticks with royal icing. Pipe some rough snow in royal icing around cake and cover with magic sparkles.

12 Roll out yellow Mexican paste on a lightly greased board. Grease letter cutters then cut out letters for 'Toys'. Brush with gold powder and attach to cake with royal icing. Confectioners varnish can be brushed over antlers, hooves, nose and candy sticks.

20cm (8in) Marzipanned cake, 28cm (11in) cake drum, 1.3kg (3lb) sugarpaste, Mexican paste, edible glue, isopropyl alcohol, one each of magic sparkle hint colours in Yellow, green, blue, pink and violet all ground finer (p1) (JK),

Paste Colours: **Eucalyptus, Egg Yellow, Ice Blue, Mint Green, Rose, Violet, Black (SF).**

Powder Colours: **Moonbeams Jade, Silver (SK).**

Bow cutters size 1, 2 & 3 (Jem), bow cutter from confetti set (PC), no.2 piping nozzle, large soft dusting brush, no.1 & 3 paintbrushes, non stick rolling board.

1 Place cake on board. Colour 900g of sugarpaste with eucalyptus. Ice cake. Use a large soft dusting brush to brush moonbeams Jade all over cake. Ice board in white sugarpaste and emboss with bow cutter.

2 For baubles colour 15g yellow, 40g blue, 25g green, 30g pink and 40g violet. Roll into smooth balls then flatten to half a ball shape. Keep the centre domed and thin the edges down.

3 Mark where the strings will be piped by measuring and marking with a cocktail stick. From the edge of the top of the cake the yellow baubles string measures 6cm, blue 10cm, green 4cm, pink 13cm, and lilac 6cm. The strings will go over the top edge of the cake and down the cake side to the board.

4 Colour a little royal icing grey and pipe strings with the no.2 nozzle. Pipe a small plain shell around base of cake. Attach baubles with royal icing.

5 Brush yellow bauble all over with glue thinly. Leave for 1 minute then apply yellow sparkles. Repeat with other baubles covering one at a time.

6 Colour some Mexican paste light grey. Grease a non stick rolling board with trex. Roll out paste, grease bow cutters and cut out bows (small for yellow, medium for pink and green, large for blue and violet). Attach the tails first then fold over and attach loops, then the knot.

7 Roll out grey Mexican paste on a greased board. Grease the small bow cutter and cut out 24 bows. Attach to cake sides with a little glue.

8 Mix isopropyl alcohol with silver powder and paint strings, piping around bottom of cake, bows on cake sides, board and baubles.

Snow Scene

20cm (8in) cake marzipanned and placed on a 30.5cm (12in) cake drum, 1.8kg (4lb) sugarpaste, 4 pots of white magic sparkles (JK), flower paste, royal icing, alcohol (gin or vodka), edible glue.

Paste Colours: Black, Spruce Green, Gooseberry, Ice Blue, Rose, Red, Chestnut Brown, paprika (SC).

Powder Colours: Snowflake Lustre, Moonbeams Jade (SK).

Side and edge smoother (Edgers), Christmas tree cutter set of 3 (PME), no.1 piping nozzle, Pizza wheel.

1 Colour 350g of sugarpaste pale grey. Roll out to an oblong shape while rolling 600g of white sugarpaste into a wider oblong. Place the two pieces long edges together and roll at the same time to get the same thickness. Roll

a little thinner than you usually would to cover a cake and enough to cover the cake and board. Overlap slightly then cut through both making a curved line with a pizza wheel. Brush cake with alcohol then place both pieces over cake so the join matches up. Smooth into cake then use the 'Edgers' smoother to smooth cake sides and board icing at the same time. Trim around edge of board.

2 Roll out 450g of sugarpaste to 3mm thick. Brush front half of cake and board with alcohol. Trim along one of the long edges in a curved line (cut it so the curve will be different to the first when laid on the cake). Place icing over cake and smooth in at sides and on board as before. Trim icing at board edges.

3 Repeat for final layer of sugarpaste rolling a slightly narrower piece. Cut a curved line again this time similar to the first one. Brush cake with alcohol then place sugarpaste over.

Smooth as before. Trim around board. The icing on the front edge of the board will look thick so finish trimmed edge with your fingers.

4 Brush top half of cake and first layer of white icing with snowflake lustre. Use a pastry brush to cover the third layer with thin glue. Cover with magic sparkles. Grind the remaining sparkles finer. Cover the second layer with glue and then the fine sparkles.

5 Place white royal icing in a piping bag with a no.1 nozzle. Pipe trees starting with trunks (pattern p36). Pipe snow onto grey sugarpaste. Pipe different size dots randomly – not spaced evenly.

6 Colour some flower paste in gooseberry and 2 shades of spruce green. Cut out different size trees in different greens. Where you want them to overlap cut a piece off with the correct size tree cutter so the fit is perfect. Dust with moonbeams jade and attach to cake.

7 The house is made from pieces of chestnut coloured sugarpaste (pattern p36). Mark some brickwork and windows with a knife. Attach a red door. The roof is made from a wedge shape piece of sugarpaste. Mix a little paste colour with water and paint curtains. Dust roof with snowflake lustre. Attach chimney and finish with a little sugarpaste for snow. Dust with snowflake lustre.

8 Using the size guide (p1), shape the snowmen from the following sizes of sugarpaste: Bodies 11, heads 8, arms 6. Dust with snowflake. Roll out small pieces of coloured sugarpaste and make hats and scarves. Mark eyes and buttons with a cocktail stick dipped in black paste colour. Add little carrot noses.

Ho Ho Ho, Pages 2-3

Sleigh Ride, Pages 12-13

Starry Night, Pages 6-7

Chocolate Time,
Mistletoe & Wine

Chocolate Time, Pages 14-15

Christmas

Greetings

Teddie's Stocking, Pages 20-21

Holly Tree, Pages 26-27

Rudolf in Toy Sack, Pages 28-29

Snow Scene, Pages 32-33